WHY A MINI SCHNAUZER?

Those seeking a hardy, lively and friendly little dog with the ability to guard and cherish his master need look no further than the Miniature Schnauzer. Here we have a big dog in a small frame, able to protect himself with great agility when called upon to do so. But it is his happy disposition, along with his intelligence, that has endeared him to dog lovers, placing him high in dogdom's popularity stakes.

His older and bigger cousins, the Giant and Standard Schnauzers, although far less popular, are highly impressive animals. They were developed from the Beaver Dog of the Middle Ages, and are renowned for their herding, hunting and guarding abilities. It was from these two, crossed probably with Affenpinschers, that the Miniature variety has been evolved during the 20th century. Today, lacking none of the great and forceful character of his ancestors, he is asserting himself ever more effectively in pet and show circles.

He has the advantage over his larger progenitors in that his compact size renders him less expensive to care for, and that he takes up so little space— so to the city dweller he seems the ideal pet. His crisp, tangle-resistant, easily cared-for, non-shedding coat makes him the meticulous housekeeper's delight. Stylish and gay in his coat and gait, he attracts attention wherever he goes, always meeting someone who, while not knowing the breed, will recognize pedigreed canine worth and inquire of his heritage. Although in German slang the word *schnauzer* means argumentative or quarrelsome, our dog's name

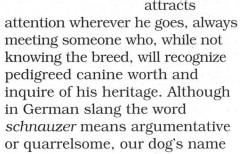
As the new owner of a Miniature Schnauzer you can look forward to many years of fun and happiness.

No one, human or canine, can resist a jar full of treats. Miniature Schnauzers are very quick to learn the rules of the house; however, some things should always be kept out of the dog's reach.

comes from the German word *schnauzbart* which means a bearded mouth.

Classified as a terrier in the United States, the Miniature Schnauzer is not considered one in Germany or England, although he has all the hunting abilities of those tough little fighters. The Standard and Giant varieties are placed in the Working Group. There can be no more rugged canine companion than the Miniature Schnauzer—with his small size he can exercise adequately in today's small apartments. His alert nature combines with a keen sense of hearing to make him a great watchdog. While not noisy or yappy, neither is the Schnauzer reticent when strangers are about; nobody, but nobody, comes in without being properly announced. He welcomes friends cheerfully and warns strangers properly.

Are there young people in the house? Friend Schnauzer will watch the baby, play dolls with the girls, or roughhouse with the boys. He will—smartly clipped—prance out fashionably with the modern Ms. or mother or hold his own rambling with father. He will do all this with admirable aplomb and self possession, switching from role to role with ease and be perfectly at home in all of them.

DESCRIPTION AND CHARACTER

The Miniature Schnauzer, "the small dog with the big personality," is a dog small in size but in no way toyish or delicate. It is surprising to many people on first picking up a Miniature Schnauzer to discover what a sturdy, heavy, muscular dog he is. He should be built with the ruggedness and power of a draft horse, combined with the elegance and beauty of a thoroughbred. Alertness, fearlessness, and adaptability to any circumstance or climate are among his chief characteristics.

His dark, medium-sized, expressive eyes, very black nose, and alert movable ears add much to his charm and appearance of extreme intelligence.

His profuse whiskers and beard, combined with his salt-and-pepper color, distinguish him from other terriers. His color can be anything from a beautiful silver gray, salt-and-pepper, to gray and pure black. The Schnauzer hair has the "agouti" pattern, each hair having all the shades of gray from almost white to black on the tips. This is what makes the salt-and-pepper color. Most dogs have hair of only one color to each hair. The whiskers, beard, and leg furnishings can be either dark or light, as long as they are confined to shades of gray. The light silver, almost white, whiskers and profuse leg hair, with a dark gray body coat, is probably the most attractive. Color is perhaps his most distinguishing mark.

The Miniature Schnauzer is a one-family dog—a very keen watchdog. He is extremely obedient and quick to learn. Alone out of doors, he will not allow a stranger to touch him; but when the same person enters the house and is

The Mini Schnauzer can easily be distinguished from other terriers by his profuse whiskers and beard combined with his salt-and-pepper coloring.

approved by the family, he accepts him without question.

He is very devoted, playful, affectionate, and, if permitted, will never let the family out of his sight. He is quick to learn when he is wanted and when to be quiet in his own bed or chair. He is equally at home in a city apartment, hotel, country estate, or farm. He can do with a small amount of exercise, yet is tireless on a weekend hiking or camping trip. He loves to swim and even has been known to get in the tub with the children. He adores walking, following a bicycle or horse, or riding in a car. He is seldom carsick and learns quickly his place in the car, and will remain quiet, not bouncing from one side to the other or hanging out the windows. Left alone in the car, he will guard it and bark only if some stranger touches it. He seldom destroys anything in the car, but sits with his alert black nose pressed against the glass awaiting his master's return.

If permitted, he likes to accompany his master to bed, either sleeping quietly on the bed or in his own bed. If his master is ill, he is tireless in his devotion, leaving his side only when absolutely required to do so, and returning as quickly as possible to his vigil.

The Miniature Schnauzer adapts easily to other animals such as cats, pet rabbits, birds, and all farm animals. Naturally, if not properly instructed at the beginning in his behavior toward them, he could learn to kill them as he does rodents. He is a good rat and mouse catcher and will dig all day after a woodchuck or groundhog. He never loses his head and fights blindly, but has enough discretion to know when he needs help with a foe too big and powerful for him alone. He is spunky and fearless, but not an aggressive fighter, so that ten or more Miniatures can run together.

The Miniature Schnauzer can be taught to notify his deaf owner when the doorbell or telephone rings, distinguish between them, and go to the bell that is ringing. He has done exceptionally well as an actor, appearing on the stage in several plays.

Miniature Schnauzers are quick to adapt to other pets you might have in your home, such as cats.

As a devoted friend, your Miniature Schnauzer will quickly learn the difference between playtime and quiet time and will also learn to act accordingly to your different moods.

BREED STANDARD

A breed standard is the criterion by which the appearance (and to a certain extent, the temperament as well) of any given dog is made subject to objective measurement. Basically, the standard for any breed is a definition of the perfect dog to which all specimens of the breed are compared. Breed standards are always subject to change through review by the national breed club for each dog, so that it is always wise to keep up with developments in a breed by checking the publications of your national kennel club. Printed below is the American Kennel Club standard for the Miniature Schnauzer.

General Appearance—The Miniature Schnauzer is a robust, active dog of terrier type, resembling his larger cousin, the Standard Schnauzer, in general appearance, and of an alert, active disposition.

Faults—Type—Toyishness, ranginess or coarseness.

Size, Proportion, Substance—**Size**—From 12 to 14 inches. He is sturdily built, nearly square in *proportion* of body length to height with plenty of bone, and without any suggestion of toyishness. *Disqualifications*—Dogs or bitches under 12 inches or over 14 inches.

Head—*Eyes* small, dark brown and deep-set. They are oval in appearance and keen in *expression. Faults*—eyes light and/or large and prominent in appearance. *Ears*—when cropped, the ears are identical in shape and length, with pointed tips. They are in balance with the head and not exaggerated in length They are set high on the skull and carried perpendicularly at the inner edges, with as little bell as possible along the outer edges. When uncropped, the ears are small and V-shaped,

The outline on the left is correct for a Miniature Schnauzer. The outline on the right is incorrect; the hindquarters are overbuilt, a common fault. Drawing by John Quinn.

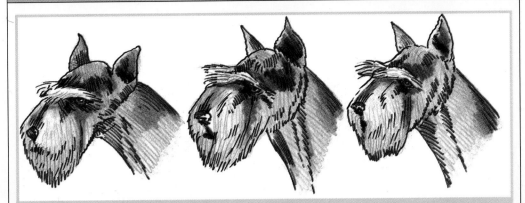

Three head types of Schnauzers: Too round and broad in the skull, and too short foreface *(left)*; correct head and ear set *(center)*; too low ear set and too light eyes *(right)*. Drawings by John Quinn.

folding close to the skull.

Head strong and rectangular, its width diminishing slightly from ears to eyes, and again to the tip of the nose. The forehead is unwrinkled. The **topskull** is flat and fairly long. The foreface is parallel to the topskull, with a slight stop, and it is at least as long as the topskull. The **muzzle** is strong in proportion to the skull; it ends in a moderately blunt manner with thick whiskers which accentuate the rectangular shape of the head. **Faults**—Head coarse and cheeky. The **teeth** meet in a **scissors bite**. That is, the upper front teeth overlap the lower front teeth in such a manner that the inner surface of the upper incisors barely touch the outer surface of the lower incisors when the mouth is closed. **Faults**—Bite—Undershot or overshot jaw. Level bite.

Neck, Topline, Body—*Neck* strong and well arched, blending into the shoulders, and with the skin fitting tightly at the throat. **Body** short and deep, with the brisket extending at least to the elbows. Ribs are well sprung and deep, extending well back to a short loin. The underbody does not present a tucked up appearance at the flank. The **backline** is straight; it declines slightly from the withers to the base of the tail. The withers form the highest point of the body. The overall length from chest to buttocks appears to equal the height at the withers. **Faults**—Chest too broad or shallow in brisket. Hollow or roach back.

Tail set high and carried erect. It is docked only long enough to be clearly visible over the backline of the body when the dog is in proper length of coat. **Fault**—Tail set too low.

Forequarters—Forelegs are straight and parallel when viewed from all sides. They have strong pasterns and good bone. They are separated by a fairly deep brisket which precludes a pinched front. The elbows are close, and the ribs spread gradually from the first rib so as to allow space for the elbows to move close to the body. **Fault**—Loose elbows. The sloping

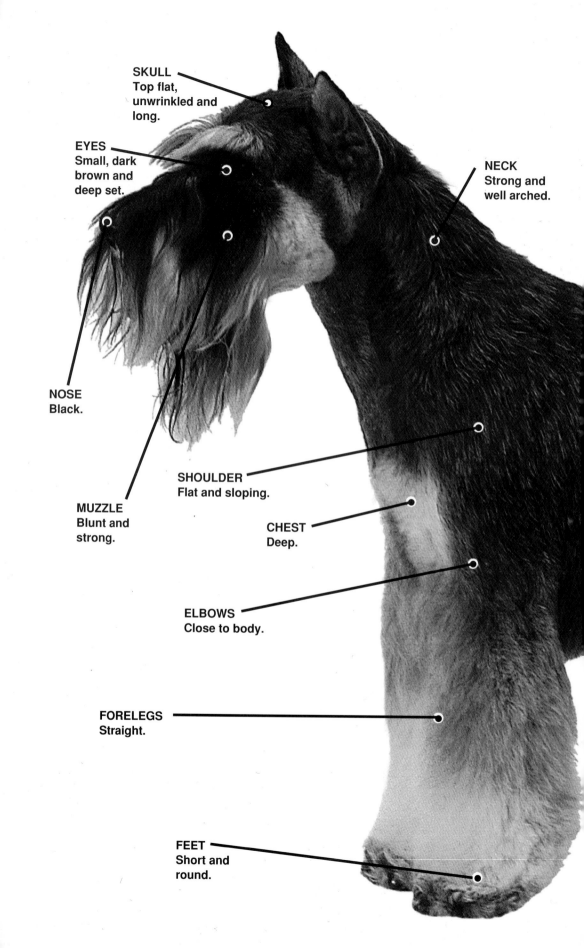

SKULL
Top flat,
unwrinkled and
long.

EYES
Small, dark
brown and
deep set.

NECK
Strong and
well arched.

NOSE
Black.

SHOULDER
Flat and sloping.

MUZZLE
Blunt and
strong.

CHEST
Deep.

ELBOWS
Close to body.

FORELEGS
Straight.

FEET
Short and
round.

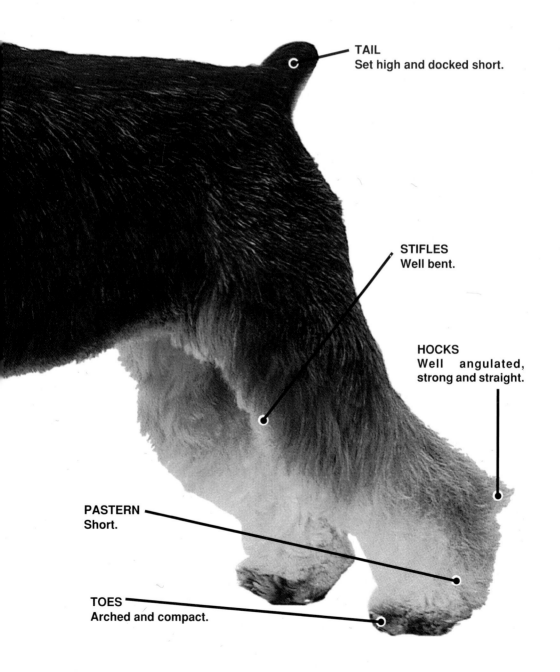

1995 Westminster Kennel Club Best of Breed winner Ch. Das Feder's Drivin Miss Daisy owned by Larry and Georgina Drivon.

TAIL
Set high and docked short.

STIFLES
Well bent.

HOCKS
Well angulated, strong and straight.

PASTERN
Short.

TOES
Arched and compact.

shoulders are muscled, yet flat and clean. They are well laid back, so that from the side the tips of the shoulder blades are in a nearly vertical line above the elbow. The tips of the blades are placed closely together. They slope forward and downward at an angulation which permits the maximum forward extension of the forelegs without binding or effort. Both the shoulder blades and upper arms are long, permitting depth of chest at the brisket. *Feet* short and round (cat

outer coat and close undercoat. The head, neck, ears, chest, tail, and body coat must be plucked. When in show condition, the body coat should be of sufficient length to determine texture. Close covering on neck, ears and skull. Furnishings are fairly thick but not silky. *Faults*—Coat too soft or too smooth and slick in appearance.

Color—The recognized colors are salt and pepper, black and silver and solid black. All colors have uniform skin pigmentation, i.e., no

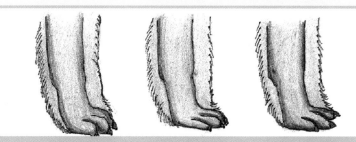

Left: Correct round feet with well-arched toes. *Center:* Flat, thin feet. *Right:* Spreading toes with weak pasterns. Drawings by John Quinn.

feet) with thick, black pads. The toes are arched and compact.

Hindquarters—The hindquarters have strong-muscled, slanting thighs. They are well bent at the stifles. There is sufficient angulation so that, in stance, the hocks extend beyond the tail. The hindquarters never appear overbuilt or higher than the shoulders. The rear pasterns are short and, in stance, perpendicular to the ground and, when viewed from the rear, are parallel to each other. *Fault*—Sickle hocks, cow hocks, open hocks or bowed hindquarters.

Coat—Double, with hard, wiry,

white or pink skin patches shall appear anywhere on the dog.

Salt and Pepper—The typical salt and pepper color of the topcoat results from the combination of black and white banded hairs and solid black and white unbanded hairs, with the banded hairs predominating. Acceptable are all shades of salt and pepper, from light to dark mixtures with tan shadings permissible in the banded or unbanded hair of the topcoat. In salt and pepper dogs, the salt and pepper mixture fades out to light gray or silver white in the eyebrows, whiskers, cheeks, under throat, inside ears, across chest, under tail, leg furnishings, and inside hind legs. It may or may not also fade out on the underbody. However, if so, the lighter underbody hair is not to rise higher on the sides of the body than the front elbows.

Black and Silver—The black and silver generally follows the same pattern as the salt and pepper. The entire salt and pepper section must be black. The black color in the topcoat of the black and silver is a true rich color with brown tinge. The scissored and clippered areas have lighter shades of black. A small white spot on the chest is permitted as is an occasional single white hair elsewhere on the body.

DISQUALIFICATIONS

Color solid white or white striping, patching, or spotting on the colored areas of the dog, except for the small white spot permitted on the chest of the black.

The body coat color in salt and

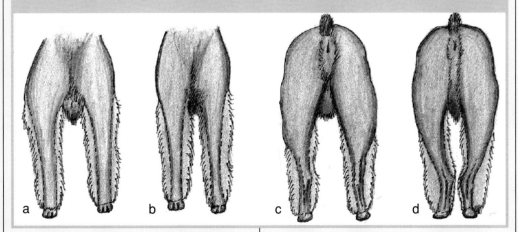

(a) Correct form with the elbows in and the legs straight. (b) The chest and front are too narrow. (c) Correct hindquarters and hocks. (d) Incorrect hindquarters—cow hocked. Drawings by John Quinn.

black undercoat. The stripped portion is free from any fading or brown tinge and the underbody should be dark.

Black—Black is the only solid color allowed. Ideally, the black color in the topcoat is a true rich glossy solid color with the undercoat being less intense, a soft matting shade of black. This is natural and should not be penalized in any way. The stripped portion is free from any fading or pepper and black and silver dogs fades out to light gray or silver white under the throat and across the chest. Between them there exists a natural body coat color. Any irregular or connecting blaze or white mark in this section is considered a white patch on the body, which is also a disqualification.

Gait—The trot is the gait at which movement is judged. When approaching, the forelegs, with elbows close to the body, move straight forward, neither too close nor too far apart. Going away, the hind legs are straight and travel in the same planes as the forelegs.

Note—*It is generally accepted that when a full trot is achieved, the rear legs continue to move in the same planes as the forelegs, but a very slight inward inclination will occur. It begins at the point of the shoulder in front and at the hip joint in the rear. Viewed from the front or rear, the legs are straight from these points to the*

Faults—Single tracking, sidegaiting, paddling in front, or hackney action. Weak rear action.

Temperament—The typical Miniature Schnauzer is alert and spirited, yet obedient to command. He is friendly, intelligent and willing to please. He should never be overaggressive or timid.

DISQUALIFICATIONS

Dogs or bitches under 12 inches or over 14 inches. Color solid white or white striping, patching, or spotting on

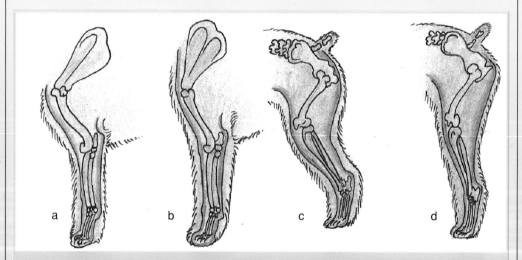

A sound dog must have a properly proportioned skeleton. (a) This is the correct structure of the shoulder required for good front angulation. (b) The shoulder shown here is too straight and steep. (c) The correct angulation for good hindquarters. (d) Incorrect angulation—the stifles are too straight. Drawings by John Quinn.

pads. The degree of inward inclination is almost imperceptible in a Miniature Schnauzer that has incorrect movement. It does not justify moving close, toeing in, crossing, or moving out at the elbows.

Viewed from the side, the forelegs have good reach, while the hind legs have strong drive, with good pickup of hocks. The feet turn neither inward nor outward.

the colored areas of the dog,

The body coat color in salt and pepper and black and silver dogs fades out to light gray or silver white under the throat and across the chest. Between them there exists a natural body coat color. Any irregular or connecting blaze or white mark in this section is considered a white patch on the body, which is also a disqualification.

Beautiful headstudy of the Best of Breed winner of the 1995 Westminster Kennel Club dog show, Ch. Das Feder's Drivin Miss Daisy owned by Larry and Georgina Drivon.

MINI SCHNAUZER HISTORY

In spite of the Miniature Schnauzer's evolvement from large stock, he breeds true to size, shape, form and outlook, a fair indication that his "manufacturers" knew what they were about. The breed can claim considerable antiquity—Durer's watercolor of 1492, "Madonna with the Many Animals" shows a typical specimen. Rembrandt showed the breed in at least one of his 17th-century works, and, in Stuttgart, a statue dated 1620 and entitled "Nightwatchman and his Dog" portrays a good and typical Schnauzer.

No one is quite sure how the Miniature form developed. Many assert that it came by selecting the smallest specimens of the Standard and consistently breeding only from the smallest offspring. However, it is probable that Affenpinschers were brought into the picture and utilized as outcrosses to small Schnauzers. In any event, that the small breed was seized up, conserved, developed and finally fixed in size and type to make the immaculate breed it is today speaks volumes for the skill and devotion of its early breeders. Since the small variety was established, it has certainly made its niche in dogdom. As a show dog it is popular, and as a working dog and companion it is first-rate.

The Miniature Schnauzer originated in Germany. Loosely translated, "schnauzer" means mustached, and the Miniature Schnauzer has a marvelous one!

FIRST REGISTRATIONS AND DEVELOPMENT

The first known registration in the breed was number 281, a black bitch whelped in October 1888, named "Findel" and owned by Herr Max Hartenstein of the then famous Plavia kennels. She was registered as being of unknown breeding, but what interests us is that she *was* registered as a *Miniature* Schnauzer, whereas prior to this time registrations were made under other breed denominations such as Miniature Pinschers and Wire-haired Miniature Pinschers, the latter being the original *Zwergschnauzers*, which we know today as Miniature Schnauzers.

picture is uncertain. What we can be sure about is that this breed, an ancient one, is not unlike the current Miniature Schnauzer in style, gait and outline.

Some people say the Affenpinscher is a progenitor of the Brussels Griffon, which is

A basket full of Affenpinscher puppies! The Affenpinscher and Standard Schnauzer were most likely the two dogs crossed to produce the Miniature Schnauzer. The resemblance surely can be seen.

Apart from "Findel," seven other bitches were registered in that period, two black, three yellow, one black-and-tan and one pepper-and-salt. Four were shown as being of unknown breeding and the others were what could be described as being of indeterminate breeding, although names were certainly specified. Clearly the background of these early Schnauzers involved Wire-haired Pinschers, Standard Schnauzers and Miniature Pinschers. Just when the Affenpinscher came into the

itself an old breed. The black of the Griffon's coat would have been inherited by the Miniature Schnauzer, for solid black was not particularly common in the Miniature Pinscher, to which breed some look as a progenitor of the Miniature Schnauzer, probably without reason.

The black has, by some, been attributed to a black Pomeranian influence on the breed, but apart from some stated effect of this breed on the Miniature Schnauzer in the Heilbroon area of Germany where blacks were bred and were

The black coloring of the Miniature Schnauzer can be traced back to either the Pomeranian or the Brussels Griffon.

popular, no other evidence of Spitz influence exists. However, it is recorded that the big Spitz breeds were used in developing the Standard Schnauzer, so if this is true it seems logical to suggest that the toy variety may have been used to form a miniature style of Schnauzer. At least one breeder has reported that a Pomeranian-type puppy turned up in a litter of purebred Miniature Schnauzers.

Like all small breeds of dogs its development encompasses a lot of supposition as to the breeds involved. Even breeds like the Fox Terrier, the Scottish Terrier, and goodness knows what else have been named as contributors. There exists a possibility that occasional infusions of other breeds have been introduced but one can be reasonably sure that if they were, their influence was sparse and of little consequence. It seems certain that the main breed influence on the Miniature Schnauzer would

have been the Affenpinscher, an attractive little dog and certainly a breed that would have contributed much in style, type, temperament, soundness, sportiness and canine character to the Miniature Schnauzer we admire today.

THE BREED IN AMERICA

Although records show that two Miniature Schnauzers were brought to the United States in 1923, when Mr. W. Goff of Concord imported a pair from Herr R. Krappatsch. This pair did not contribute much to the breed, the dog dying without progeny and the bitch from the Goldbachhöhe kennels producing only two litters.

The kennels of Mrs. Marie E. Slattery (then Mrs. Marie E. Lewis)

Many different breeds have influenced the Mini Schnauzer. Like all small breeds of dog, its development encompasses a lot of supposition. Whatever the true background, the Mini Schnauzer is a big dog in a small package!

Kismet of Marienhof, from Marie Slattery's famed kennel of the 1930s, sired two American champion daughters.

can claim to have commenced serious Miniature Schnauzer breeding with four imports from the same Herr Krappatsch. This occurred in 1924 and the following year the first homebred (American) litter was recorded by Mrs. Slattery, whose famous Marienhof kennels produced some wonderful early Miniature Schnauzer champions. About the same time Mrs. Slattery imported her starting stock, some other dogs were brought in and it is believed that about 150 imports were made during the subsequent decade. Most were registered at the American Kennel Club and quite a number were bred from, certainly the best were used. Today, American Miniature Schnauzer championship winning stock traces back to about a dozen dogs and the same number of bitches from these original imports!

Probably the most important Miniature Schnauzer as far as America is concerned is one who never set foot in the country! This is Fels von den Goldbachhöhe, whose son, Mack von den Goldbachhöhe, and two daughters, Lady and Lotte von den Goldbachhöhe out of Amsel von den Goldbachhöhe, show up in pedigrees time and time again; their combined influence on the breed is clearly an excellent one. The sisters did better than the unfortunate Mack who died after siring a few litters.

The first Miniature Schnauzer to be registered at the American Kennel Club was Mr. Monson Morris's Borste von Bischofsleben, but unfortunately no champion stock came from this bitch to honor the Woodway kennels. During the early years, most Schnauzers (even the Standards) were known as Wire-haired Pinschers and they were relegated to the Working

Marienhof Kennels' Ch. Cockerel of Sharvogue, one of three brothers who were very famous in the Miniature Schnauzer world of the 1930s. Owned by Marie Slattery, Cockerel sired five American and two Canadian champions.

Group classes. A club—the Wire-haired Pinscher Club of America—catered to the enthusiasts, but in 1926, the breed became known by its current name of Schnauzer. Standards and Miniatures were shown together until 1927, when separate classes for the two sizes were held at the Combined Terrier Club's show. At this point confusion arose as to whether the breed and its sizes should be classified in the Terrier or Working Groups.

Later, in 1933, the Miniature enthusiasts were successful in founding a Club, while the organization called the Standard Schnauzer Club of America specialized in the larger variety. This move was forced upon the fancy by virtue of a move by the American Kennel Club to view both sizes of Schnauzers without distinction, purely as one breed. Had such a ruling been accepted, it would have meant that the two varieties would have been interbred, to the probable detriment of both, a situation not to be contemplated by the breed pioneers who had done so much work to separate the two sizes.

The Standard Schnauzer, shown here, and the Miniature Schnauzer were at one time exhibited together. Had the two classes not been separated, the two varieties would have probably been interbred...detrimental to both breeds.

EARLY SCHNAUZERS IN AMERICA

Most interest in the breed started after World War I. "Resy Patricia" from Switzerland became the first champion. Sieger "Holm von Egelsee" was imported form Germany and won an American championship without much trouble. Mrs. M. Newton then bred Champion "Fracas Franconia" from "Resy Patricia". Seven years after the Great War, the Schnauzer Club of America was formed, but as public interest appeared to be divided between the Standard and Miniature varieties, it soon became evident that two distinct clubs were needed to look after the separate and specific interests of each. And so, the American Miniature Schnauzer Club was formed in 1933. The original club continued under the name of the Standard Schnauzer Club of America and was concerned only with the larger dog.

It was a far cry from the days when the big Schnauzer existed only as a yard or stable dog; he had now achieved a high position in dogdom where his size, strength and canine beauty were admired.

YOUR NEW PUPPY

SELECTION

When you do pick out a Mini Schnauzer puppy as a pet, don't be hasty; the longer you study puppies, the better you will understand them. Make it your transcendent concern to select only one that radiates good health and spirit and is lively on his feet, whose eyes are bright, whose coat shines, and who comes forward eagerly to make and to cultivate your acquaintance. Don't fall for any shy little darling that wants to retreat to his bed or his box, or plays coy behind other puppies or people, or hides his head under your arm or jacket appealing to your protective instinct. *Pick the Mini Schnauzer puppy who forthrightly picks you! The feeling of attraction should be mutual!*

Before you bring your new puppy home, everything should be in place for its arrival. His bed should be ready and all accessories purchased so that his move is not any more traumatic than it has to be.

DOCUMENTS

Now, a little paper work is in order. When you purchase a purebred Mini Schnauzer puppy, you should receive a transfer of ownership, registration material, and other "papers" (a list of the immunization shots, if any, the puppy may have been given; a note on whether or not the puppy has been wormed; a diet and feeding schedule to which the puppy is accustomed) and you are welcomed as a fellow owner to a long, pleasant association with a most lovable pet, and more (news)paper work.

GENERAL PREPARATION

You have chosen to own a particular Mini Schnauzer puppy. You have chosen it very carefully over all other breeds and all other puppies. So before you ever get that Mini Schnauzer puppy home, you will have prepared for its arrival by reading everything you can get your hands on having to do with the management of Mini Schnauzers and puppies. True, you will run into many conflicting opinions, but at least you will not

A crate will benefit your Mini Schnauzer in many ways. First, it will act as a den and provide security, and second, it helps a great deal in housebreaking.

Wrapped in a towel and carried in the arms or lap of a passenger, the Mini Schnauzer puppy will usually make the trip without mishap. If the pup starts to drool and to squirm, stop the car for a few minutes. Have newspapers handy in case of car-sickness. A covered carton lined with newspapers provides protection for puppy and car, if you are driving alone. Avoid excitement and unnecessary handling of the puppy on arrival. A Mini Schnauzer puppy is a very small "package" to be making a complete change of surroundings and company, and he needs frequent rest and refreshment to renew his vitality.

be starting "blind." Read, study, digest. Talk over your plans with your veterinarian, other "Mini Schnauzer people," and the seller of your Mini Schnauzer puppy.

When you get your Mini Schnauzer puppy, you will find that your reading and study are far from finished. You've just scratched the surface in your plan to provide the greatest possible comfort and health for your Mini Schnauzer; and, by the same token, you do want to assure yourself of the greatest possible enjoyment of this wonderful creature. You must be ready for this puppy mentally as well as in the physical requirements.

TRANSPORTATION

If you take the puppy home by car, protect him from drafts, particularly in cold weather.

Shredded paper is often used as bedding while the puppies are with their dam. You may want to include some shredded paper in your puppy's bed when you bring it home.

THE FIRST DAY AND NIGHT

When your Mini Schnauzer puppy arrives in your home, put him down on the floor and don't pick him up again, except when it is absolutely necessary. He is a dog, a real dog, and must not be lugged around like a rag doll. Handle him as little as possible, treatment. Be calm, friendly, and reassuring. Encourage him to walk around and sniff over his new home. If it's dark, put on the lights. Let him roam for a few minutes while you and everyone else concerned sit quietly or go about your routine business. Let the puppy come

Select a Mini Schnauzer puppy that radiates good health, a shiny coat, and bright eyes.

and permit no one to pick him up and baby him. To repeat, *put your Mini Schnauzer puppy on the floor or the ground and let him stay there except when it may be necessary to do otherwise.*

Quite possibly your Mini Schnauzer puppy will be afraid for a while in his new surroundings, without his mother and littermates. Comfort him and reassure him, but don't console him. Don't give him the "oh-you-poor-itsy-bitsy-puppy" back to you.

Playmates may cause an immediate problem if the new Mini Schnauzer puppy is to be greeted by children or other pets. If not, you can skip this subject. The natural affinity between puppies and children calls for some supervision until a live-and-let-live relationship is established. This applies particularly to a Christmas puppy, when there is more excitement than usual and more chance for a puppy to swallow something upsetting. It is a better plan to welcome the puppy several days before or after the holiday week. Like a baby, your Mini Schnauzer puppy needs much rest and should not be over-handled. Once a child realizes that a puppy has "feelings" similar to his own, and can readily be hurt or injured, the opportunities for play and responsibilities provide exercise and training for both.

For his first night with you, he should be put where he is to sleep every night—say in the kitchen, since its floor can usually be easily cleaned. Let him explore the kitchen to his heart's content; close doors to confine him there. Prepare his food and feed him lightly the first night. Give him a pan with some water in it—not a lot, since most puppies will try to drink the whole pan dry. Give him an old coat or shirt to lie on. Since a coat or shirt will be strong in human scent, he will pick it out to lie on, thus furthering his feeling of security in the room where he has just been fed.

To aid in housebreaking, save a piece of paper that your puppy has "puddled" on and place it where you always want him to go. Your puppy will seek out this spot, because of its smell, and will return to it every time.

HOUSEBREAKING HELPS

Now, sooner or later—mostly sooner—your new Mini Schnauzer puppy is going to "puddle" on the floor. First take a newspaper and lay it on the puddle until the urine is soaked up onto the paper. *Save this paper.* Now take a cloth with soap and water, wipe up the floor and dry it well. Then take the wet paper and place it on a fairly large square of newspapers in a convenient corner. When cleaning up, always keep a piece of wet paper on top of the others. Every time he wants to "squat," he will seek out this spot and use the papers. (This routine is rarely necessary for more than three days.) Now leave your Mini Schnauzer puppy for the night. Quite probably he will cry and howl a bit; some are more stubborn than others on this matter. But let him stay alone for the night. This may seem harsh treatment, but it is the best procedure in the long run. Just let him cry; he will weary of it sooner or later.

MINI SCHNAUZER GROOMING

This need not be an arduous task, especially if you keep your dog in good hard muscular condition and maintain the quality of his coat by correct feeding. Nor is a great deal of equipment necessary, but that which is should be selected with care. On no account should a dog come to dislike the daily brushing and grooming process. It should always recommended for stripping. But do not use it until the coat is longer. A steel comb will also be needed. It will remove much of the unwanted dead body hair or loosen it so that it can be pulled out by a twist of the fingers.

DAILY GROOMING

Brushing once a day is essential. If you do it regularly, the chore will

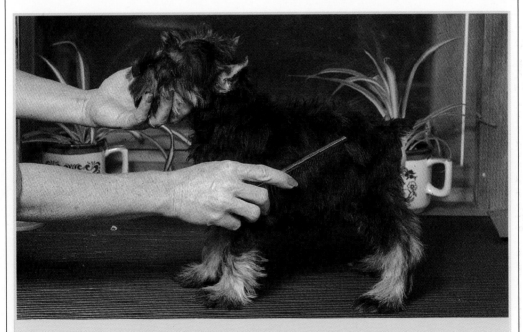

Brushing your Mini Schnauzer once a day is essential for a healthy coat.

be a pleasant period in which you get to know your dog, and he gets to know you—a time to develop mutual confidence and affection.

GROOMING TOOLS

A soft bristle brush is better for the puppy. Later, he will need a wire bristle of the type take only a few minutes. Make yourself comfortable while you're doing the grooming. Put the dog on a table or sit beside him on the floor. Be sure to roll him over to brush his underparts but be careful not to scratch the tender skin. First, brush with the growth of the hair to clean the

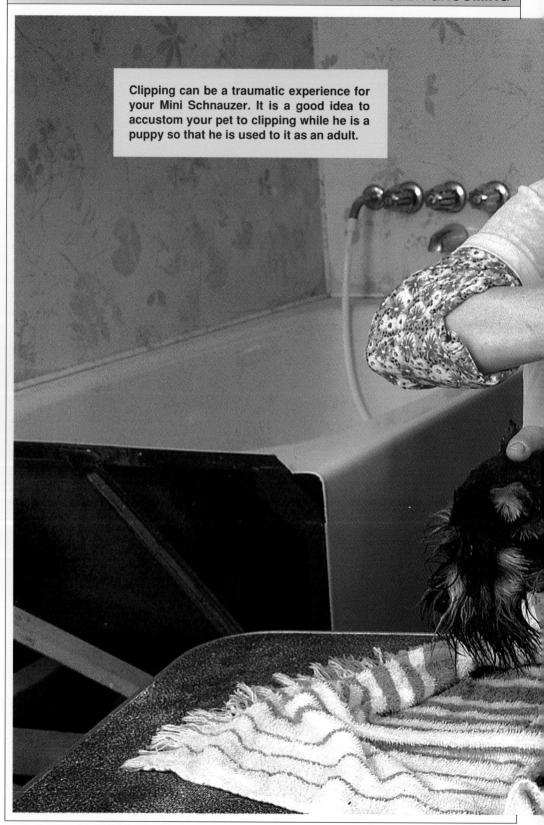

Clipping can be a traumatic experience for your Mini Schnauzer. It is a good idea to accustom your pet to clipping while he is a puppy so that he is used to it as an adult.

surface coat. Then brush stiffly against the growth to clean the undercoat and massage the skin. Last, brush the hair back to its original position. Use the metal comb on the eyebrows and whiskers and on mats if any should be encountered. When combing out a mat of hair, grasp a tuft at the base and tease it out with the end of the comb—*do not pull against the skin.* During daily brushing the Schnauzer's coat and ears should always be

a bath. Obviously, if he is unquestionably dirty or has encountered some noxious substance in his travels, the job will have to be done.

Morning is the best time. Then there is sure to be plenty of sunshine to help dry the dog. However, if you have already fed him in the morning, let a couple of hours elapse before the bath. And give the dog a chance to relieve himself before you begin. Make sure that everything you

When bathing your Mini Schnauzer, be careful not to let water get into the ears. Place cotton balls in the ears before you begin the bathing process to avoid such mishaps.

checked for parasites. Blunt-end scissors can be used to snip off any wild hairs.

THE BATH

It is inadvisable to bathe any dog frequently; the bath removes the natural oils. A dog bathed too often can always be detected by his indifferent coat. If your Schnauzer is brushed and groomed daily he will rarely need

will need is within reach, especially if you are working by yourself, because the average Schnauzer does not like baths and will try to climb out of the tub if left alone.

The water should be warm, but not hot. The dog's own body temperature—101.2°F—is about right. It is a good idea to put a rubber mat on the bottom of the tub or sink to keep the dog from slipping. Have at least two good-sized Turkish towels—beach towels are good—handy, because, before you're done, there will be plenty of water to soak up.

Unless it is a hot summer's day, try to avoid bathing the dog outdoors. Even under the best of conditions he may become chilled. And after the bath keep him in a warm room until he is thoroughly dry. In fact, it is wise to postpone a bath until the right conditions exist— on a damp day, a chilly house can prove disastrous.

There are an untold number of dog soaps and shampoos on the market. A medicated shampoo is probably best. There are also some that are good for parasites if your dog has hitch-hiker problems. It is not a good idea to use household

Thoroughly dry your puppy or dog after its bath to avoid its becoming chilled and consequently ill.

When properly combed, the whiskers and the beard of your Miniature Schnauzer are distinguishing characteristics.

detergents or laundry soap; they are too harsh and inappropriate for a dog's coat. Think more in terms of bathing a baby than of washing a car.

A portable rubber shower spray will be useful. If no shower spray is at hand, use a sprinkling can. In that case, at least two warm water rinses will have to be standing waiting before you begin.

Plug the dog's ears with cotton, and rub a little petroleum jelly on the eyelids to keep the soap out of the eyes.

Wet the dog and work the shampoo well into his coat, right

him; if not you will be caught off guard as he gives a tremendous shake. If you are in a work area where a small shower doesn't matter, protect yourself with the towel and let the dog shake himself vigorously. Then towel him as dry as possible, rubbing down to the skin, not just wiping off the surface dampness.

A hair dryer can be used in the final drying, as it is important to dry the dog as quickly as possible. While hand dryers are satisfactory, those on stands are even better since they leave both hands free to brush the dog's hair out as it

A portable shower spray is useful when bathing your dog.

down to the skin. That is where the dirt is. Start at the tail and work forward. Save the head until last. When you get to the head, do not use soap or shampoo. Wipe it off with an unsoaped damp cloth. Rinse thoroughly and repeat. Some owners even give their dog a third going-over.

As you lift the dog from the tub after the final rinsing, have a big bath towel ready to wrap around

dries. Be especially careful about the feet; see that no dampness is left between the toes or under the tail. This also applies to the ears; be doubly sure that no moisture has penetrated into the inner ear.

It is a rare Schnauzer that enjoys a bath so it is wise to make sure that the whole proceeding is made as pleasant as possible. Talk to the dog soothingly all through it. The first bath is

Bonding with your puppy is important. Grooming sessions can be used as additional bonding opportunities.

and after such a venture, the eyes should be washed out with a commercial dog eye wash, or if none is at hand, lukewarm water. Some owners recommend a mild boric acid solution (2%) but this writer does not use it—too many dogs have had their eyes injured by boric acid.

Eyes that are constantly rheumy and watering are suspect, and a veterinarian should be consulted. It may be the result of entropion, a hereditary condition in which the eyelids turn inward, or ectropion, when they turn outward. However, simple conjunctivitis—inflamed and watering eyes—can usually be dealt with at home. There are several reliable preparations on the market to combat it. Sometimes the gentle rubbing of sterile cod liver oil on the upper

particularly important. A puppy, however, should not be bathed until it is at least six months old. Before then, it can be kept clean with one of the dry dog shampoos that are on the pet market, following instructions on the container. These too can be used for the older dog if the weather is inclement, or conditions are such that a tub bath is not practical.

EYE CARE

The eyes frequently collect foreign matter like seeds and pollen when the dog roams through high grass or ground cover. These can be irritating,

Clean the outer portion of your Mini Schnauzer's ear with a cotton swab dipped in peroxide or alcohol.

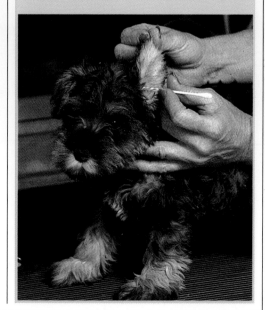

and lower eyelid helps. Any mucus in the eye corners can be removed with a cotton-tipped swab dipped in lukewarm water.

EAR CARE

Daily ear examination is always wise. Never wash out a dog's ears with soap and water—not even the outer ear. If water gets deep into the ear, it is almost impossible to get it out, and it can present all kinds of problems. The best way to clean ears is with a cotton swab dipped in peroxide, alcohol or olive oil. Never probe deeper into the ear than you can see. If it seems unusually sensitive, or has a foul smell, it is wise to consult your vet. There are several good medicated dog earwashes on the market. Ask your favorite pet shop owner to recommend one.

Also be wary of ear canker, which is a common infection in Schnauzers.

NAIL CLIPPING

The Schnauzer's paw should be what is known in dogdom as cat-like. This means that the nails must always be as short as

The condition of your Miniature Schnauzer's teeth must be checked for tartar build-up on a regular basis. A Nylabone® is critical to help to maintain your Schnauzer's teeth.

possible. If the dog does not keep them worn down by active exercise on hard pavements, you will have to clip them regularly. Do not try to use human nail clippers; they crush the dog's thick nail. They can, of course, be used to nip off the sharp curved tips of a puppy's nails, but for the older dog the guillotine-type nail clipper is preferred. Be especially careful not to cut into the quick, the soft spongy area of flesh whose blood vessels feed the nail. If this is cut, the wound will bleed profusely, although not dangerously. The blood can be stanched with a styptic pencil or powdered alum, or by pressing the injured foot into a dish of sugar. However, it is wise to be careful since it will pain the dog and leave him leery of nail trimming. Any rough edges can be filed off with a heavy-duty file or rasp, working from the base of the nail toward the tip.

FOOT CARE

When grooming the dog, it is wise to check the foot-pads. They can easily become sore, punctured by splinters or thorns, or cut by broken glass; burrs can become wedged between the toes. Remove the foreign object, flush out the wound with a jet of water, and encourage the dog to lick it. Tar and gum can be removed from the pads and hair of the feet with acetone. If that isn't handy, try nail polish remover.

TRIMMING AND STRIPPING

If the coat of the Miniature Schnauzer is left uncared for, it will, before long, take on a bizarre appearance that makes the dog look like another breed. Schnauzers are stripped and trimmed for neatness to show off their best features and reveal their strong lines. The Schnauzer's hair, growing unkempt as it often does, can mar his sturdy handsomeness. For instance, too much hair on the skull can give him a coarse appearance; too much hair on the neck can make it look too thick; bunched hair in the wrong places can spoil the lines.

Of course, care must be taken not to overdo the stripping and trimming; otherwise the dog will look all wrong. This is why I take a dim view of grooming the Schnauzer with an electric clipper, a fairly common practice today.

Routine nail care is essential to your Miniature Schnauzer's good health. Puppy nails are especially sharp and need to be tended to often.

There is no question that dog trimming is an art. Skill can come only with practice. The beginner should, if he possibly can, watch a professional groomer at work on some Schnauzer, if not his own. With practice, the knack is not too difficult to acquire.

These are three ways to strip a Schnauzer. The correct one is by hand stripping. With this method, the dog's coat, which is usually salt and pepper or tones of black and gray, does not "change color" because the outer coat is not clipped off. The dog is merely neatened up to look trim and perky.

The second method is with the use of what is known as a stripping knife. This is sometimes used by professional groomers because it is faster. Its results are similar to those of hand stripping and while it cuts the hair, changing the dog's color to some degree, it is an easier device for the novice to use.

The third way is with an electric dog clipper. The various widths of blades in the clipper give the effect of stripping but since a great deal of hair is removed, right down to the skin, the color change is sometimes startling. It is a method frequently used in dog beauty salons for the pet Schnauzer. It has the advantage of speed but it cannot be used on the show dog.

While all three methods are acceptable, I recommend hand stripping. Although it is more tedious and time consuming, the owner who wants his pet always looking its best will employ it. And if he does not care to strip the dog himself, he will insist upon hand striping by the professional groomer.

The Mini Schnauzer's coat is a high maintenance job. Choose the best grooming tools from your local pet shop. Photo courtesy of Wahl Clipper.

STRIPPING EQUIPMENT

Stripping Knife: The stripping knife is a small serrated knife with various width spacings between the teeth. The best stripping knives come from England, France, and Germany. There is also a more complicated version of the stripping knife, utilizing a razor blade. Knives and dressers are available in pet shops. Hand stripping can also be done with forefinger and thumb, but only skilled groomers ever attempt it.

Chalk: This is used to get a firm grip on the hair to make it easier to pluck. Any brand of French chalk is satisfactory.

A well-groomed Mini Schnauzer is a pleasant sight to behold. Here we see one patiently waiting for his handler's return to complete the grooming job.

Scissors: Two pairs are needed. A small one about 4 inches long with rounded tips, it is used to get into the ears as they must not be left with any stray hairs, inside or out. A longer pair of barber scissors, 7 or 8 inches, is used for the finishing touches and for edging.

Comb: A steel comb or special - inch terrier comb is advisable—one with fine teeth at one end and coarse open teeth at the other.

HAND STRIPPING

Unlike the Poodle, which can be trimmed in a variety of styles, there is only one correct style for the Schnauzer—a neat, square box-like look. The amount of hair to be removed is optional, some like it long, some short. However, if the dog is being groomed for show purposes, the coat should be left fairly long but given an orderly, finished look.

Professional groomers require a sturdy table on which to place the dog. A good overhead light that does not cast any shadows is also essential to a proper clipping.

Brush: This is used to remove dead hair; it should have fine short wire bristles of steel set in a rubber backing for resiliency. It will give a nice luster and finish.

The equipment needed also includes a sturdy table placed under a very good light that casts as few shadows as possible. The top of the table should be covered with a non-slip rubber mat.

Stand the dog on the table, facing forward. Chalk the area on which you are working. Standing at his side, get a good grip on his skin. Start from the neck and work in the opposite direction with the knife, plucking the hair by pinching it with the thumb pressed against the knife and twisting it away from the body. It is an action similar to that of plucking feathers from a chicken.

Do not belabor one area but follow rapidly the contour of the neck, shoulders and body. The quicker you twist off the hair, the less discomfort it will cause the dog. It will also keep you from creating bald patches.

Follow the contour of the neck blending somewhat heavier as you approach the withers (shoulders) and getting heavier as you work along the rib cage area. A slight fringe of hair should be left at the base of the ribs and loin but it should not be too prominent; it should taper into the tuck-up, which is the area between the loin and thigh.

The rump, loin and stifle (knee joint) should be stripped shorter than the body down to the hock

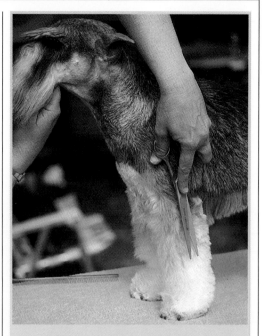

The proper way to clip your Miniature Schnauzer can be learned from a professional groomer. This dog is having his legs trimmed, note the clipping is being done in a downward motion.

A Mini Schnauzer's leg is groomed to look as nearly as possible like a "barber pole."

joint. The hair should flair out from the hock with full fringing. Use scissors to trim the edges and around the paws.

The head which is the focal point of the Schnauzer should have a fresh, alert and feisty look. This is accomplished by stripping quite closely between the ears, around the cheeks and above the eyes, and at the corners of the mouth under the throat, to the pith of the neck.

The whiskers should start at the base of the outer corner of the eye and fall forward toward the mouth and nose. The whiskers should not be trimmed directly below the eyes but a little hair should be plucked from between the eyes to give a quizzical look.

When the Mini Schnauzer is thoroughly dry, the legs are to be recombed and scissored.

This expression can be heightened by using the long scissors, cutting in a slanting position from the outer corner of the eye toward the inner corner (very slightly) giving a fine edge to the eyebrows. The whiskers can be scissored with a slight edging to create a boxy look. The ears are scissored clean with the round-tip scissors on the inside as well as the back and base of the ear with the edges of the ears scissored.

The legs are left with as much hair as possible with only the edges trimmed neatly and the paws rounded at the base to give a cat-like "up on the toes" look. The insides of the legs should be thinned out, but not too close to the skin The chest should be blended into the abdomen with no feathers or fringe jutting out from the body. Nor should there be any

suggestion of chaps or shoulder pads as with the Poodle; instead the shoulder should blend into the elbow. The tail is stripped to the length of the body rounded on the end with no fringe at the rear or base of tail.

When you have finished the stripping, comb and brush the Schnauzer thoroughly to remove any loose hairs. Double check to make sure that the coat is even and that you have left no gashes or tufts of hairs sticking out. The scissors can be used for the finishing touches to give the dog an overall boxy, cobby, square-headed appearance.

ELECTRIC CLIPPER

The third method of stripping the Schnauzer is with a small animal electric clipper, such as sold in pet shops. Many diverse trims can be

Your Mini Schnauzer's first experience with an electric clipper can be very traumatic. Be sure to talk soothingly to him the entire time and be gentle but firm in your approach.

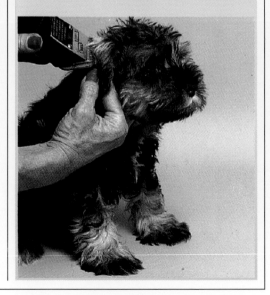

made with this instrument. The Schnauzer can be given a very short haircut, a medium one, or one that is cleverly disguised to give a hand-stripped look. This method is, of course, faster than the other two. The clipper used must be the kind that uses interchangeable blades or heads. The #7 or #5 blade has wide-spaced teeth that leave about one

The ears can be shaved with these blades, but extreme care should be taken since the tips of the ears are so narrow that they can be cut by the fast-moving blades. It is better to use scissors. The #15 blade works exceptionally close; it takes most of the dog's hair off the body and leaves the skin showing. This really makes the dog's hair look

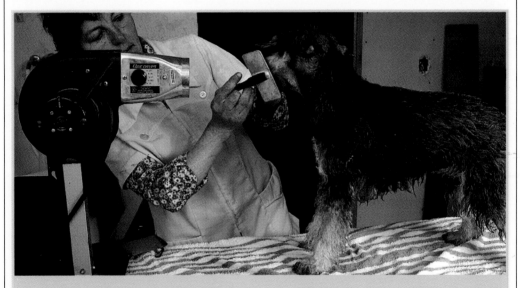

To keep your Miniature Schnauzer's beard looking its best, it must be combed, brushed and conditioned—always kept clean and never allowed to mat.

half inch of hair on the body making it appear hand stripped. Nor does the color change too much, but it will be a little lighter since the top hairs are clipped off in a stronger way than with the dresser or stripping knife. The pattern is the same as for hand stripping, and so is the scissoring. The blade more commonly used in a #10, which cuts closer than the #5 or #7 leaving about one quarter inch of hair. This blade will alter the color several shades lighter.

light and many owners at first don't recognize their pets because of this sudden color change. This blade (#15) is not recommended. It gives the Schnauzer a completely alien look.

Whatever method you use on your dog, always remember to be patient but firm since the Schnauzer is a breed with a fidgety temperament. He is not an easy animal to groom—not at all like the Poodle who adores the attention of a beauty parlor.

FEEDING

Now let's talk about feeding your Mini Schnauzer, a subject so simple that it's amazing there is so much nonsense and misunderstanding about it. Is it expensive to feed a Mini Schnauzer? No, it is not! You can feed your Mini Schnauzer accustomed to. Many dogs flatly refuse to eat nice, fresh beef. They pick around it and eat everything else. But meat—bah! Why? They aren't accustomed to it! They'd eat rabbit fast enough, but they refuse beef because they aren't used to it.

You don't have to be a gourmet chef to feed your Miniature Schnauzer properly. You can feed your dog economically and keep him in perfect shape the year 'round without a lot of fuss. These puppies are waiting patiently for their meal.

economically and keep him in perfect shape the year round, or you can feed him expensively. He'll thrive either way, and let's see why this is true.

First of all, remember a Mini Schnauzer is a dog. Dogs do not have a high degree of selectivity in their food, and unless you spoil them with great variety (and possibly turn them into poor, "picky" eaters) they will eat almost anything that they become

VARIETY NOT NECESSARY

A good general rule of thumb is forget all human preferences and don't give a thought to variety. Choose the right diet for your Mini Schnauzer and feed it to him day after day, year after year, winter and summer. But what is the right diet?

Hundreds of thousands of dollars have been spent in canine nutrition research. The results are pretty conclusive, so you needn't go into a lot of experimenting with trials of this and that every other week. Research has proven just what your dog needs to eat and to keep healthy.

DOG FOOD

There are almost as many right diets as there are dog experts, but the basic diet most often recommended is one that consists of a dry food, either meal or kibble

Do not choose any food in which the protein level is less than 25 percent, and be sure that this protein comes from both animal and vegetable sources. The good dog foods have meat meal, fish meal, liver, and such, plus protein from alfalfa and soy beans, as well as some dried-milk product. Note the vitamin content carefully. See that they are all there in good proportions; and be especially

There are several excellent quality dog foods available on the market that are manufactured by reliable companies.

form. There are several of excellent quality, manufactured by reliable companies, research tested, and nationally advertised. They are inexpensive, highly satisfactory, and easily available in stores everywhere in containers of five to 50 pounds. Larger amounts cost less per pound, usually.

If you have a choice of brands, it is usually safer to choose the better known one; but even so, carefully read the analysis on the package.

certain that the food contains properly high levels of vitamins A and D, two of the most perishable and important ones. Note the B-complex level, but don't worry about carbohydrate and mineral levels. These substances are plentiful and cheap and not likely to be lacking in a good brand.

The advice given for how to choose a dry food also applies to moist or canned types of dog foods, if you decide to feed one of these.

For no-mess feeding, a feeding tray is very practical. Feeding trays are available in different styles and colors at your local pet shop. Photo courtesy of Penn Plax.

Having chosen a really good food, feed it to your Mini Schnauzer as the manufacturer directs. And once you've started, stick to it. Never change if you can possibly help it. A switch from one meal or kibble-type food can usually be made without too much upset; however, a change will almost invariably give you (and your Mini Schnauzer) some trouble.

WHEN SUPPLEMENTS ARE NEEDED

Now what about supplements of various kinds, mineral and vitamin, or the various oils? They are all okay to add to your Mini Schnauzer's food. However, if you are feeding your Mini Schnauzer a correct diet, and this is easy to do, no supplements are necessary unless your Mini Schnauzer has been improperly fed, has been sick, or is having puppies. Vitamins and minerals are naturally present in all the foods; and to ensure against any loss through processing, they are added in concentrated form to the dog food you use. Except on the advice of your veterinarian, added amounts of vitamins can prove harmful to your Mini Schnauzer! The same risk goes with minerals.

FEEDING SCHEDULE

When and how much food to give your Mini Schnauzer? As to when (except in the instance of puppies), suit yourself. You may feed two meals per day or the same amount in one single feeding, either morning or night. As to how to prepare the food and how much to give, it is generally best to follow the directions on the food package. Your own Mini Schnauzer may want a little more or a little less.

Fresh, cool water should always be available to your Mini Schnauzer. This is important to good health throughout his lifetime.

ALL MINI SCHNAUZERS NEED TO CHEW

Puppies and young Mini Schnauzers need something with resistance to chew on while their teeth and jaws are developing—for cutting the puppy teeth, to induce growth of the permanent teeth under the puppy teeth, to assist in

Your Mini Schnauzer will enjoy chewing on a Gumabone® during the day for relaxation and smart dental pacification.

hambone scented
GUMABONE®
POOCH PACIFIER

GIANT-SIZE

"WHY"
On Reverse Side

The Nylabone/Gumabone® Pooch Pacifiers enable the dog to slowly chew off the knobs while they clean their own teeth. The knobs develop elastic frays which act as a toothbrush. These pacifiers are extremely effective, as detailed scientific studies have shown.

dollars when their chewing instinct is not diverted from their owner's possessions. And this is why you should provide your Mini Schnauzer with something to chew—something that has the necessary functional qualities, is desirable from the Mini Schnauzer's viewpoint, and is safe for him.

It is very important that your Mini Schnauzer not be permitted to chew on anything he can break or on any indigestible thing from which he can bite sizable chunks. Sharp pieces, such as from a bone which can be broken by a dog, may pierce the intestinal wall and kill. Indigestible things that can be bitten off in chunks, such as from shoes or rubber or plastic toys, may cause an intestinal stoppage (if not regurgitated) and bring painful death, unless surgery is promptly performed.

Strong natural bones, such as 4- to 8-inch lengths of round shin bone from mature beef—either the kind you can get from a butcher or one of the variety available commercially in pet stores—may

getting rid of the puppy teeth at the proper time, to help the permanent teeth through the gums, to ensure normal jaw development, and to settle the permanent teeth solidly in the jaws.

The adult Mini Schnauzer's desire to chew stems from the instinct for tooth cleaning, gum massage, and jaw exercise—plus the need for an outlet for periodic doggie tensions.

This is why dogs, especially puppies and young dogs, will often destroy property worth hundreds of

Chocolate Nylabone® has a one micron thickness coat of chocolate under the skin of the nylon. When the Miniature Schnauzer chews it, the white subsurface is exposed. This photo shows before and after chewing.

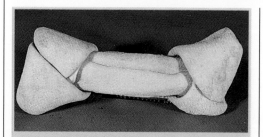

Rawhide is probably the best selling dog chew. It can be dangerous and cause a dog to choke on it as it swells when wet. A molded, melted rawhide mixed with casein is available (though always scarce), which is the safer option for your Miniature Schnauzer.

serve your Mini Schnauzer's teething needs if his mouth is large enough to handle them effectively. You may be tempted to give your Mini Schnauzer puppy a smaller bone and he may not be able to break it when you do, but puppies grow rapidly and the power of their jaws constantly increases until maturity. This means that a growing Mini Schnauzer may break one of the smaller bones at any time, swallow the pieces, and die painfully before you realize what is wrong.

A chicken-flavored Gumabone® has tiny particles of chicken powder embedded in it to keep the Miniature Schnauzer interested.

All hard natural bones are very abrasive. If your Mini Schnauzer is an avid chewer, natural bones may wear away his teeth prematurely; hence, they then should be taken away from your dog when the teething purposes have been served. The badly worn, and usually painful, teeth of many mature dogs can be traced to excessive chewing on natural bones.

Contrary to popular belief, knuckle bones that can be chewed up and swallowed by your

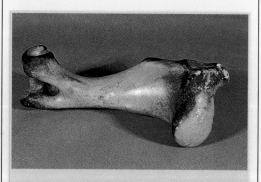

Pet shops sell real bones which have been colored, cooked, dyed or served natural. Some of the bones are huge, but they usually are easily destroyed and become very dangerous.

Mini Schnauzer provide little, if any, usable calcium or other nutrient. They do, however, disturb the digestion of most dogs and cause them to vomit the nourishing food they need.

Dried rawhide products of various types, shapes, sizes, and prices are available on the market and have become quite popular. However, they don't serve the primary chewing functions very well; they are a bit messy when wet from mouthing, and most

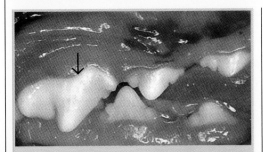

In a scientific study, this shows a dog's tooth while being maintained by Gumabone® chewing.

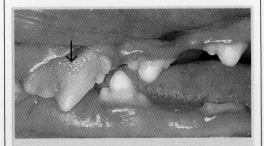

The Gumabone® was taken away and in 30 days the tooth was almost completely covered with plaque and tartar.

Mini Schnauzers. The melting process also sterilizes the rawhide. Don't confuse this with pressed rawhide, which is nothing more than small strips of rawhide squeezed together.

The nylon bones, especially those with natural meat and bone fractions added, are probably the most complete, safe, and economical answer to the chewing need. Dogs cannot break them or bite off sizable chunks; hence, they are completely safe—and being longer lasting than other things offered for the purpose, they are economical.

The nylon tug toy is actually a dental floss. You grab one end and let your Miniature Schnauzer tug on the other as it slowly slips through his teeth since nylon is self-lubricating (slippery). Do NOT use cotton rope tug toys as cotton is organic and rots. It is also weak and easily loses strands which are indigestible if swallowed.

Mini Schnauzers chew them up rather rapidly—but they have been considered safe for dogs until recently. Now, more and more incidents of death, and near death, by strangulation have been reported to be the results of partially swallowed chunks of rawhide swelling in the throat. More recently, some veterinarians have been attributing cases of acute constipation to large pieces of incompletely digested rawhide in the intestine.

A new product, molded rawhide, is very safe. During the process, the rawhide is melted and then injection molded into the familiar dog shape. It is very hard and is eagerly accepted by

REDUCES TARTAR BUILD-UP DOGS' TEETH

PLAQUE ATTACKER

DENTAL FLOSS

EXERCISER

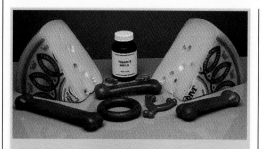

Pet shops sell dog treats which are healthy and nutritious. Cheese is added to chicken meal and other high-protein foods to be melted together and molded into hard chew devices or pacifiers. Don't waste your money on low-protein treats. If the pacifier doesn't have at least a 50% protein content, pass it up!

Hard chewing raises little bristle-like projections on the surface of the nylon bones—to provide effective interim tooth cleaning and vigorous gum massage, much in the same way your toothbrush does it for you. The little projections are raked off and swallowed in the form of thin shavings, but the chemistry of the nylon is such that they break down in the stomach fluids and pass through without effect.

The toughness of the nylon provides the strong chewing resistance needed for important jaw exercise and effectively aids teething functions, but there is no tooth wear because nylon is non-abrasive. Being inert, nylon does not support the growth of microorganisms; and it can be washed in soap and water or it can be sterilized by boiling or in an autoclave.

Nylabone® is highly recommended by veterinarians as a safe, healthy nylon bone that can't splinter or chip. Nylabone®

is frizzled by the dog's chewing action, creating a toothbrush-like surface that cleanses the teeth and massages the gums. Nylabone®, the only chew products made of flavor-impregnated solid nylon, are available in your local pet shop. Nylabone® is superior to the cheaper bones because it is made of virgin nylon, which is the strongest and longest-lasting type of nylon available. The cheaper bones are made from recycled or re-ground nylon scraps, and have a tendency to break apart and split easily.

Nothing, however, substitutes for periodic professional attention for your Mini Schnauzer's teeth and gums, not any more than your toothbrush can do that for you. Have your Mini Schnauzer's teeth cleaned at least once a year by your veterinarian (twice a year is better) and he will be happier, healthier, and far more pleasant to live with.

Most pet shops have complete walls dedicated to safe pacifiers.

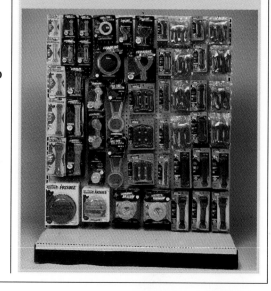

Nylabone® products are safe chewing devices for your Miniature Schnauzer, puppy or adult. Be sure to provide your puppy with plenty of Nylabone® products to satisfy its chewing needs.

TRAINING

You owe proper training to your Mini Schnauzer. The right and privilege of being trained is his birthright; and whether your Mini Schnauzer is going to be a handsome, well-mannered housedog and companion, a show dog, or whatever possible use he may be put to, the basic training mannerly in the presence of other dogs. He must not bark at children on roller skates, motorcycles, or other domestic animals. And he must be restrained from chasing cats. It is not a dog's inalienable right to chase cats, and he must be reprimanded for it.

Miniature Schnauzers have proven very capable of achieving degrees in obedience. Obedience trials are very much enjoyed by the dogs as well as their owners.

is always the same—all must start with basic obedience, or what might be called "manner training."

Your Mini Schnauzer must come instantly when called and obey the "Sit" or "Down" command just as fast; he must walk quietly at "Heel," whether on or off lead. He must be mannerly and polite wherever he goes; he must be polite to strangers on the street and in stores. He must be

PROFESSIONAL TRAINING

How do you go about this training? Well, it's a very simple procedure, pretty well standardized by now. First, if you can afford the extra expense, you may send your Mini Schnauzer to a professional trainer, where in 30 to 60 days he will learn how to be a "good dog." If you enlist the services of a good professional trainer, follow his advice of when to come to see the dog. No, he won't forget you, but too-frequent visits at the wrong time may slow down his training progress. And using a "pro" trainer means that you will have to go for some training, too, after the trainer feels your Mini Schnauzer is ready to go home. You will have to learn how your Mini Schnauzer works, just what to expect of him and how to use what the dog has learned after he is home.

OBEDIENCE TRAINING CLASS

Another way to train your Mini Schnauzer (many experienced Mini Schnauzer people think this is the best) is to join an obedience training class right in your own community. There is such a group in nearly every community nowadays. Here you will be working with a group of people who are also just starting out. You will actually be training your own dog, since all work is done under the direction of a head trainer who will make suggestions to you and also tell you when and how to correct your Mini Schnauzer's errors. Then, too, working with such a group, your Mini Schnauzer will learn to get

All dogs should be trained to obey the rules of the house. If your pet is never permitted on the furniture, do not give in, not even once. Rules that are allowed to be broken are seldom obeyed.

along with other dogs. And, what is more important, he will learn to do exactly what he is told to do, no matter how much confusion there is around him or how great the temptation is to go his own way.

Write to your national kennel club for the location of a training club or class in your locality. Sign up. Go to it regularly—every session! Go early and leave late! Both you and your Mini Schnauzer will benefit tremendously.

TRAIN HIM BY THE BOOK

The third way of training your Mini Schnauzer is by the book. Yes, you can do it this way and do a good job of it too. But in using the book method, select a book, buy it, study it carefully; then study it some more, until the procedures are almost second nature to you. Then start your training. But stay with the book and its advice and exercises. Don't start in and then make up a few rules of your own. If you don't follow the book, you'll get into jams you can't get out of by yourself. If after a few hours of short training sessions your Mini Schnauzer is still not working as he should, get back to the book for a study session, because it's your fault, not the dog's! The procedures of dog training have been so well systemized that it must be your fault, since literally thousands of fine Mini Schnauzers have been trained by the book.

After your Mini Schnauzer is "letter perfect" under all conditions, then, if you wish, go on to advanced training and trick work.

Your Mini Schnauzer will love his obedience training, and you'll burst with pride at the finished product! Your Mini Schnauzer will enjoy life even more, and you'll enjoy your Mini Schnauzer more. And remember—you *owe good training to your Mini Schnauzer.*

There are certain commands that every well-behaved Mini Schnauzer should know. This dog is learning the "down/stay" command.

SHOWING YOUR MINI SCHNAUZER

A show Mini Schnauzer is a comparatively rare thing. He is one out of several litters of puppies. He happens to be born with a degree of physical perfection that closely approximates the standard by which the breed is judged in the show ring. Such a dog should, on maturity, be able to win or approach his championship in good, fast company at the larger shows. Upon finishing his

competitive sport. While all the experts were once beginners, the odds are against a novice. You will be showing against experienced handlers, often people who have devoted a lifetime to breeding, picking the right ones, and then showing those dogs through to their championships. Moreover, the most perfect Mini Schnauzer ever born has faults, and in your hands the faults will be far more evident than with the experienced

A Miniature Schnauzer with a strong champion bloodline and who, of course, closely matches the standard for the breed, has a very good chance of becoming a champion himself.

championship, he is apt to be as highly desirable as a breeding animal. As a proven stud, he will automatically command a high price for service.

Showing Mini Schnauzers is a lot of fun—yes, but it is a highly

handler who knows how to minimize his Mini Schnauzer's faults. These are but a few points on the sad side of the picture.

The experienced handler, as I say, was not born knowing the ropes. He learned—*and so can*

Be patient with your struggle for a good show dog. It takes a lot of hard work and devotion on both your part and on your dog's.

you! You can if you will put in the same time, study and keen observation that he did. But it will take time!

KEY TO SUCCESS

First, search for a truly fine show prospect. Take the puppy home, raise him by the book, and as carefully as you know how, give him every chance to mature into the Mini Schnauzer you hoped for. My advice is to keep your dog out of big shows, even Puppy Classes, until he is mature. Maturity in the male is roughly two years; with the female, 14 months or so. When your Mini Schnauzer is approaching maturity, start out at match shows, and, with this experience for both of you, then go gunning for the big wins at the big shows.

Next step, read the standard by which the Mini Schnauzer is judged. Study it until you know it by heart. Having done this, and while your puppy is at home (where he should be) growing into a normal, healthy Mini Schnauzer, go to every dog show you can possibly reach. Sit at the ringside and watch Mini Schnauzer judging. Keep your ears and eyes open. Do your own judging, holding each of those dogs against the standard, which you now know by heart.

In your evaluations, don't start looking for faults. Look for the virtues—the best qualities. How does a given Mini Schnauzer shape up against the standard? Having looked for and noted the virtues, then note the faults and see what prevents a given Mini Schnauzer from standing

Show-quality dogs must have their coats kept in the very best condition at all times.

correctly or moving well. Weigh these faults against the virtues, since, ideally, every feature of the dog should contribute to the harmonious whole dog.

"RINGSIDE JUDGING"

It's a good practice to make notes on each Mini Schnauzer, always holding the dog against

Schnauzers and not others. Listen while the judge explains his placings, and, I'll say right here, any judge worthy of his license should be able to give reasons.

When you're not at the ringside, talk with the fanciers and breeders who have Mini Schnauzers. Don't be afraid to

Before actually entering a show it is a good idea to attend as many shows as possible and try to evaluate the dogs yourself. Compare your selection with the judge and afterwards talk to the judge's and find out why he chose certain Mini Schnauzers and not others.

the standard. In "ringside judging," forget your personal preference for this or that feature. What does the standard say about it? Watch carefully as the judge places the dogs in a given class. It is difficult from the ringside always to see why number one was placed over the second dog. Try to follow the judge's reasoning. Later try to talk with the judge after he is finished. Ask him questions as to why he placed certain Mini

ask opinions or say that you don't know. You have a lot of listening to do, and it will help you a great deal and speed up your personal progress if you are a good listener.

THE NATIONAL CLUB

You will find it worthwhile to join the national Mini Schnauzer club and to subscribe to its magazine. From the national club, you will learn the location of an approved regional club near you. Now, when your young Mini Schnauzer is eight to ten months old, find out the dates of match shows in your section of the country. These differ from regular shows only in that no championship points are given. These shows are especially designed to launch young dogs

keep your eye on the judge to see what he may want you to do next. Watch only the judge and your Mini Schnauzer. Be quick and be alert; do exactly as the judge directs. Don't speak to him except to answer his questions. If he does something you don't like, don't say so. And don't irritate the

Miniature Schnauzers prove highly trainable and athletic as can be seen in this photo of a Mini Schnauzer jumping over a brick wall obstacle in an agility trial.

(and new handlers) on a show career.

ENTER MATCH SHOWS

With the ring deportment you have watched at big shows firmly in mind and practice, enter your Mini Schnauzer in as many match shows as you can. When in the ring, you have two jobs. One is to see to it that your Mini Schnauzer is always being seen to its best advantage. The other job is to

judge (and everybody else) by constantly talking and fussing with your dog.

In moving about the ring, remember to keep clear of dogs beside you or in front of you. It is my advice to you *not* to show your Mini Schnauzer in a regular point show until he is at least close to maturity and after both you and your dog have had time to perfect ring manners and poise in the match shows.

YOUR MINI SCHNAUZER'S HEALTH

We know our pets, their moods and habits, and therefore we can recognize when our Miniature Schnauzer is experiencing an off-day. Signs of sickness can be very obvious or very subtle. As any mother can attest, diagnosing and treating an ailment require common sense, knowing when to seek home remedies and when to visit your doctor...or veterinarian, as the case may be.

Your veterinarian, we know, is your Miniature Schnauzer's best friend, next to you. It will pay to be choosy about your veterinarian. Talk to dog-owning friends whom you respect. Visit more than one vet before you make a lifelong choice. Trust your instincts. Find a knowledgeable, compassionate vet who knows Miniature Schnauzers and likes them.

Grooming for good health makes good sense. The Miniature Schnauzer's coat has a thick undercoat with a harsh outer coat that requires specific care. Plucking and clippering may need to be done every two or three months, particularly on the show dog. Regular brushing stimulates the natural oils in the coat and also removes dead haircoat. Miniature Schnauzers shed seasonally, which means their undercoat (the soft downy white fur) is pushed out by the incoming new coat. A medium-strength bristle brush helps to move the dead undercoat along.

Your Miniature Schnauzer will be a friend and companion to you for many years. You owe it to your pet to provide the very best care and to seek veterinary assistance should he fall ill.

ANAL SACS

Anal sacs, sometimes called anal glands, are located in the musculature of the anal ring, one on either side. Each empties into the rectum via a small duct. Occasionally their secretion becomes thickened and accumulates so you can readily feel these structures from the outside. If your Miniature Schnauzer is scooting across the floor dragging

Just as a mother is aware when her child is feeling ill, an owner should be able to detect when his pet is not well. A difference in appetite, personality and/or facial expression are usually the first signs that a dog is not feeling well.

kidneys, and eyes. The breed can suffer from a keratinization disorder known as Schnauzer comedo syndrome which is characterized by scaling on the skin and chronic blackheads. This type of seborrhea is probably due to hypothyroidism or an allergy though veterinarians commonly prescribe medicated shampoos to help manage the condition.

Kidney and urinary tract "stones" (called calculi or uroliths) occur in Schnauzers, most commonly containing

The undisputed champion of dog health books is Dr. Lowell Ackerman's encyclopedic work *Owner's Guide to DOG HEALTH*. It covers every subject that any dog owner might need. It actually is a complete veterinarian's handbook in simple, easy-to-understand language with hundreds of color photographs to illustrate the disease processes.

his rear quarters, or licking his rear, his anal sacs may need to be expressed. Placing pressure in and up towards the anus, while holding the tail, is the general routine. Anal sac secretions are characteristically foul-smelling, and you could get squirted if not careful. Veterinarians can take care of this during regular visits and demonstrate the cleanest method.

MAJOR HEALTH ISSUES

Many Miniature Schnauzers are predisposed to certain congenital and inherited abnormalities that affect the skin, urinary tract,

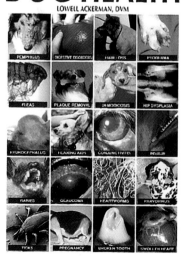

magnesium ammonium phosphate hexhydrate (or MAP). Vets advise against supplementing vitamin C in Miniature Schnauzers for this reason.

The Mini Schnauzer's eyes have become a concern to present-day breeders, recording occurrence of juvenile cataracts, as well as retinal degeneration, kerato corrected by a specialist and time is of the utmost importance. Since juvenile cataracts is linked hereditarily, breeders are extremely careful to screen for the defect. It can occur in a litter many generations removed from the affected ancestor, so screening must be thorough.

Von Willebrand's disease, a bleeding disorder, is a condition

Your pet Miniature Schnauzer will enjoy all the comforts of home when not feeling well.

conjunctivitis sicca and progressive retinal atrophy. Screening for eye problems, therefore, has been prioritized. Retinal dysplasia like PRA is an inherited defect that can severely reduce a dog's vision. Juvenile cataracts is the most serious eye problem for Miniature Schnauzers today. Certain affected dogs will contract a "hot eye" within two or three days, if this is not treated within five days the dog will suffer total blindness. It can be that affects many dog breeds and does not exclude the Miniature Schnauzer. The breed also may suffer from Legg-Perthes disease, which affects the hip joint; usually one leg is involved as well. Legg-Perthes disease most commonly affects the small breeds of dogs, just as hip dysplasia affects the larger breeds.

Hypothyroidism (malfunction of the thyroid gland) can be linked to many symptoms in Miniature

Schnauzers, such as keratinization disorders, obesity, lethargy, and reproductive disorders. Supplementation of the thyroid decreases problems, though such dogs should likely not be bred.

Despite this lengthy list of potential problems, a well-bred Miniature Schnauzer is a healthy,

and geography. The basic vaccinations to protect your dog are: parvovirus, distemper, hepatitis, leptospirosis, adenovirus, parainfluenza, coronavirus, bordetella, tracheobronchitis (kennel cough), Lyme disease and rabies.

Parvovirus is a highly

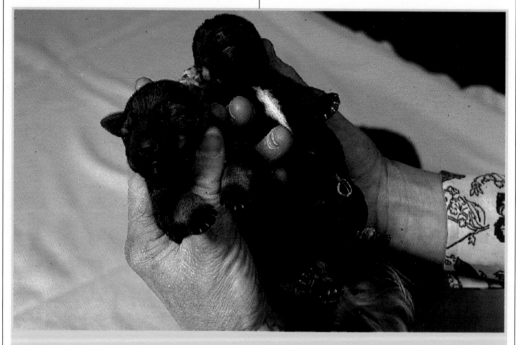

Puppies should not be handled until after their first set of vaccinations at six weeks of age, which includes a parvo shot.

long-lived companion animal. Proper care and education can only help owners promote the health and longevity of their dogs.

VACCINATIONS

For the continued health of your dog, owners must attend to vaccinations regularly. Your veterinarian can recommend a vaccination schedule appropriate for your dog, taking into consideration the factors of climate

contagious, dog-specific disease, first recognized in 1978. Targeting the small intestine, parvo affects the stomach, and diarrhea and vomiting (with blood) are clinical signs. Although the dog can pass the infection to other dogs within three days of infection, the initial signs, which include lethargy and depression, don't display themselves until four to seven days. When affecting puppies under four weeks of age, the heart muscle is frequently attacked. When the heart is affected, the puppies exhibit difficulty in breathing and experience crying and foaming at the nose and mouth.

Distemper, related to human measles, is an airborne virus that spreads in the blood and ultimately in the nervous system and epithelial tissues. Young dogs or dogs with weak immune systems can develop encephalomyelitis (brain disease) from the distemper infection. Such dogs experience seizures, general weakness and rigidity, as well as "hardpad." Since distemper is largely incurable, prevention through vaccination is vitally important. Puppies should be vaccinated at six to eight weeks of age, with boosters at ten to 12 weeks. Older puppies (16 weeks and older) who are unvaccinated should receive no fewer than two

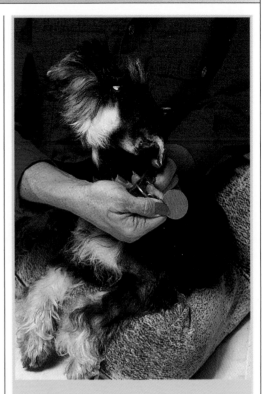

It is a good idea to keep your pet Schnauzer's rabies vaccination tag attached to its collar in case he accidentally runs away from home so that no one treats the dog unjustly.

Your Miniature Schnauzer's health should be maintained from puppyhood through adulthood.

vaccinations at three- to four-week intervals.

Hepatitis mainly affects the liver and is caused by canine adenovirus type I. Highly infectious, hepatitis often affects dogs nine to 12 months of age. Initially the virus localizes in the dog's tonsils and then disperses to the liver, kidney and eyes. Generally speaking the dog's immune system is capable of combating this virus. Canine infectious hepatitis affects dogs whose systems cannot fight off the adenovirus. Affected dogs have fever, abdominal pains, bruising on mucous membranes and gums, and experience coma and convulsions. Prevention of hepatitis exists only through vaccination at eight to ten weeks of age and then boosters three or four weeks later, then annually.

Leptospirosis is a bacterium-related disease, often spread by rodents. The organisms that spread leptospirosis enter through the mucous membranes and spread to the internal organs via the bloodstream. It can be passed through the dog's urine. Leptospirosis does not affect young dogs as consistently as the other viruses; it is reportedly regional in distribution and somewhat dependent on the immunostatus of the dog. Fever, inappetence, vomiting, dehydration, hemorrhage, kidney and eye disease can result in moderate cases.

Bordetella, called canine cough, causes a persistent hacking cough in dogs and is very contagious. Bordetella involves a virus and a bacteria: parainfluenza is the most common virus implicated; *Bordetella bronchiseptica,* the bacterium. Bronchitis and pneumonia result in less than 20 percent of the cases, and most dogs recover from the condition within a week to four weeks. Non-prescription medicines can help relieve the hacking cough, though nothing can cure the condition before it's run its course. Vaccination cannot guarantee protection from canine cough, but it does ward off the most common virus responsible for the condition.

Lyme disease (also called borreliosis), although known for decades, was only first diagnosed in dogs in 1984. Lyme disease can

There are many plants that are poisonous to dogs. Supervise your Mini Schnauzer whenever he is outdoors and don't let him nibble on leaves or berries.

Fleas thrive in warm grassy areas and can become pesty if not detected immediately. Loss of hair and habitual biting and chewing rank among the annoyances of flea infestation.

affect cats, cattle, and horses, but especially people. In the U.S., the disease is transmitted by two ticks carrying the *Borrelia burgdorferi* organism: the deer tick (*Ixodes scapularis*) and the western black-legged tick (*Ixodes pacificus*), the latter primarily affects reptiles. In Europe, *Ixodes ricinus* is responsible for spreading Lyme. The disease causes lameness, fever, joint swelling, inappetence, and lethargy. Removal of ticks from the dog's coat can help reduce the chances of Lyme, though not as much as avoiding heavily wooded areas where the dog is most likely to contract ticks. A

vaccination is available, though it has not been proven to protect dogs from all strains of the organism that cause the disease.

Rabies is passed to dogs and people through wildlife: in North America, principally through the skunk, fox and raccoon; the bat is not the culprit it was once thought to be. Likewise, the common image of the rabid dog foaming at the mouth with every hair on end is unlikely the truest scenario. A rabid dog exhibits difficulty eating, salivates much and has spells of paralysis and awkwardness. Before a dog reaches this final state, it may experience anxiety, personality changes, irritability and more aggressiveness than is usual. Vaccinations are strongly recommended as rabid dogs are too dangerous to manage and are commonly euthanized. Puppies are generally vaccinated at 12 weeks of age, and then annually. Although rabies is on the decline in the world community, tens of thousands of humans die each year from rabies-related incidents.

COPING WITH PARASITES

Parasites have clung to our pets for centuries. Despite our modern efforts, fleas still pester our pet's existence, and our own. All dogs itch, and fleas can make even the happiest dog a miserable, scabby mess. The loss of hair and habitual biting and chewing at themselves rank among the annoyances; the nuisances include the passing of tapeworms and the whole family's itching through the summer months. A full range of flea-control and elimination products are available at pet shops, and your veterinarian surely has recommendations. Sprays, powders, collars and dips fight fleas from the outside; drops and pills fight the good fight from inside. Discuss the possibilities with your vet. Not all products can be used in conjunction with one another, and some dogs may be more sensitive to certain applications than others. The dog's living quarters must be debugged as well as the dog itself. Heavy infestation may require multiple treatments.

Always check your dog for ticks carefully. Although fleas can be acquired almost anywhere, ticks are more likely to be picked up in heavily treed areas, pastures or other outside grounds (such as dog shows or obedience or field trials). Athletic, active, and hunting dogs are the most likely subjects, though any passing dog can be the host. Remember Lyme disease is passed by tick infestation.

As for internal parasites, worms are potentially dangerous for dogs and people. Roundworms, hookworms, whipworms, tapeworms, and heartworms comprise the blightsome party of troublemakers. Deworming puppies begins at around two to three weeks and continues until three months of age. Proper hygienic care of the environment is also important to prevent contamination with roundworm and hookworm eggs. Heartworm preventatives are recommended by most veterinarians, although there are some drawbacks to the regular introduction of poisons into our dogs' system. These daily or monthly preparations also help regulate most other worms as well. Discuss worming procedures with your veterinarian.

Roundworms pose a great threat to dogs and people. They are found in the intestine of dogs, and can be passed to people through ingestion of feces-contaminated dirt. Roundworm infection can be prevented by not walking dogs in heavy-traffic people areas, by burning feces, and by curbing dogs in a responsible manner. (Of course, in most areas

Be sure to provide your Miniature Schnauzer with plenty of fresh cold water at all times. There are water bottles that attach to the sides of crates to supply water freely while your dog is confined.

of the country, curbing dogs is the law.) Roundworms are typically passed from the bitch to the litter, and the bitch should be treated along with the puppies, even if she tested negative prior to whelping. Generally puppies are treated every two weeks until two months of age.

Hookworms, like roundworms, are also a danger to dogs and people. The hookworm parasite amounts of blood in the places where the worms latch onto the dog's intestines, etc.

Although infrequently passed to humans, whipworms are cited as one of the most common parasites in America. These elongated worms affect the intestines of the dog, where they latch on, and cause colic upset or diarrhea. Unless identified in stools passed,

Prior to a puppy's first set of vaccinations, the only antibodies it has are those of its mother.

(known as *Ancylostoma caninum*) causes cutaneous larva migrans in people. The eggs of hookworms are passed in feces and become infective in shady, sandy areas. The larvae penetrate the skin of the dog, and the dog subsequently becomes infected. When swallowed, these parasites affect the intestines, lungs, windpipe, and the whole digestive system. Infected dogs suffer from anemia and lose large whipworms are difficult to diagnose. Adult worms can be eliminated more consistently than the larvae, since whipworms exhibit unusual life cycles. Proper hygienic care of outdoor grounds is critical to the avoidance of these harmful parasites.

Tapeworms are carried by fleas, and enter the dog when the dog swallows the flea. Humans can acquire tapeworms in the same way, though we are less likely to swallow fleas than dogs are. Recent studies have shown that certain rodents and other wild animals have been infected with tapeworms, and dogs can be affected by catching and/or eating these other animals. Of course, outdoor hunting dogs and terriers are more likely to be infected in this way than are your typical house dog or non-motivated hound. Treatment for tapeworm has proven very effective, and infected dogs do not show great discomfort or symptoms. When people are infected, however, the liver can be seriously damaged. Proper cleanliness is the best bet against tapeworms.

Heartworm disease is transmitted by mosquitoes and badly affects the lungs, heart and blood vessels of dogs. The larvae of *Dirofilaria immitis* enters the dog's bloodstream when bitten by an infected mosquito. The larvae takes about six months to mature. Infected dogs suffer from weight loss, appetite loss, chronic coughing and general fatigue. Not all affected dogs show signs of illness right away, and carrier dogs may be affected for years before clinical signs appear. Treatment of heartworm disease has been effective but can be dangerous also. Prevention as always is the desirable alternative. Ivermectin is the active ingredient in most heartworm preventatives and has proven to be successful. Check with your veterinarian for the preparation best for your dog. Dogs generally begin taking the preventatives at eight months of age and continue to do so throughout the non-winter months.

The great outdoors can be dangerous to your Miniature Schnauzer. Fleas and ticks can be picked up by your dog, so check him over carefully as soon as he comes back indoors.

SUGGESTED READING

The following books are all published by T.F.H. Publications, Inc. and are recommended to you for additional information:

Successful Dog Training by Michael Kamer (TS-205) contains the latest training methods used by professional dog trainers. Author and Hollywood dog trainer Michael Kamer is one of the most renowned trainers in the country, having trained both stunt dogs for movies and house pets for moviestars such as Frank Sinatra, Barbara Streisand, Arnold Schwarzenegger, Sylvester Stallone, and countless others. The most modern techniques of training are presented step-by-step and illustrated with fantastic full-color photography. Whether you are a long time obedience trainer or a new dog owner, *Successful Dog Training* will prove an invaluable tool in developing or improving your own training skills.

Canine Lexicon by Andrew DePrisco and James Johnson, (TS-175) is an up-to-date encyclopedic dictionary for the dog person. It is the most complete single volume on the dog ever published covering more breeds than any other book as well as other relevant topics, including health, showing, training, breeding, anatomy, veterinary terms, and much more. No dog book before has ever offered this many stunning color photographs of all breeds, dog sports, and topics (over 1300 in full color).

The Book of the Miniature Schnauzer by Anna Katherine Nicholas (H-1080), is filled with information on the breed all over the world, standards for the breed, selection, care, grooming, showing breeding and health. With more than 100 full-color photographs, this is a must for Miniature Schnauzer owners.

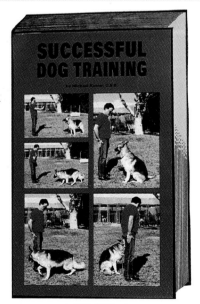

TS-205

H-1080